THE FIRST WORLD WAR

Conrad Mason

Designed by Karen Tomlins

History consultant: Terry Charman,
Imperial War Museum

Reading consultant: Alison Kelly,
Roehampton University

Edited by Jane Chisholm

Photographic manipulation by Keith Furnival

First published in 2010 by Usborne Publishing Ltd., Usborne House, 83-85 Saffron Hill, London EC1N 8RT, England. www.usborne.com Copyright © 2013, 2010 Usborne Publishing Ltd.

Acknowledgements

© AKG-IMAGES pp12-13, p60(t); © ALAMY front cover (Andrii Mykhailov), p15 (Classic Image), p27(m) (David Wall), p29(br) (The Art Archive), p31, p34 (Classic Image), p35 (The Art Archive), p37(tr), p42 (The Art Archive), p55 (The Art Archive); © THE ART ARCHIVE pp24-25 (Australian War Memorial), pp52-53 (Australian War Memorial); © CORBIS p9 (Christel Gerstenberg), p11 (Keystone), p14 (Bettmann), pp20-21(b) (Hulton-Deutsch Collection), p27(t) (George Hall), p32, p44, p46(m), p50(t) (Bettmann), p52 (Imperial War Museum), p57 (Hulton-Deutsch Collection), p58 (Bettmann), p60(b) (Bettmann); © GETTY IMAGES front cover (Hulton Archive), p7 (Imagno/Hulton Archive) p5(t) (Time Life Pictures) (b), p16 (ND/Roger Viollet), p18 (Hulton Archive), p22(b) (Hulton Archive), pp28-29 (MPI/Hulton Archive), p29(bl) (Hulton Archive), p33 (JJ Marshall/Hulton Archive), p35(t) (Popperfoto), p36 (Hulton Archive), pp46-47 (FPG/Hulton Archive), pp50-51 (Henry Guttmann/Hulton Archive), p61 (Hugo Jaeger/Time & Life Pictures), pp62-63 (David Hughes/Robert Harding World Imagery); © IMPERIAL WAR MUSEUM, LONDON, back cover adapted from (Q2756), p1 (Q5100), pp2-3 (Q743), p4(b) (Q81831), p5(b) (Q91840), p7(t) (Q81824), pp8-9 (Q22084), p17 (Q5817), p21(t) (Q23732), p26 (HU89191), p37(b) (Q754), p38 (Q70168), p39 (E(AUS) 1220), p41(b) (Ho 43), p43 (PST2734), p48 (Q47997), p49 (Q8618), p54(b) (Q58939), p56 (Q433225) p63 (Q42446), p64 (Q2756); © TOPFOTO p8(t), pp30-31 (Imperial War Museum), p41(t) (Topham Picturepoint), p45 (The Granger Collection); © WALLSTEIN VERLAG p23 (Armin T Wegner)

Many of the photographs in this book were originally in black and white and have been digitally tinted by Usborne Publishing.

Title page: Scottish soldiers climb out of a trench to attack, on the Western Front.

Contents

Fresh-faced British soldiers march into battle, confident of victory.

Chapter 1
Murder in Sarajevo

On a bright summer's morning in 1914, Archduke Franz Ferdinand of Austria and his wife Sophie were driving through Sarajevo, in Bosnia.

In their open-topped car, they enjoyed the cool breeze and the warm sunshine, and the cheers of the crowds that lined their route. They had no idea that their lives were in danger.

Without warning, a young Bosnian stepped from the crowd and hurled a bomb at the Archduke's car. It bounced off and hit the car behind, injuring several people.

Archduke Franz Ferdinand and his wife outside the town hall in Sarajevo.

The would-be assassin of Franz Ferdinand is caught by Austrian police.

The Archduke and his wife were shaken, but relieved to be alive. They carried on to the town hall, where Ferdinand was due to give a speech.

On the way back, the driver took a wrong turn, past a shop where a teenager had just bought a sandwich. The teenager was Gavrilo Princip, another assassin. Hardly believing his luck, he pulled out a pistol and fired two shots.

"Sophie, don't die!" begged the Archduke. But it was too late. Within minutes, he and his wife were dead.

Gavrilo Princip was arrested at once. But his crime would set the world aflame.

Gavrilo Princip, shown here, died of tuberculosis in prison, in 1918.

Chapter 2
The balance of power

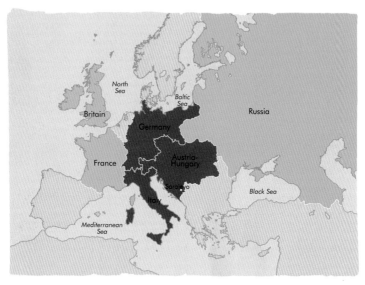

This map shows Europe in September, 1914. The 'great powers' – Germany, Britain, France, Russia, Italy and Austria-Hungary – had split into two opposing groups, shown in red and green.

Franz Ferdinand had been the heir to the Austro-Hungarian Empire. This was one of Europe's 'great powers' – alongside Germany, Britain, France, Russia and Italy. As the 20th century dawned, there had been peace between these nations for 30 years. But it was an unhappy peace.

Many of the great powers were nervous of Germany. It had only become a single nation in 1871, when it was formed out of a collection of small states. Now its proud ruler, Kaiser Wilhelm II, was determined to make Germany as powerful as any other nation in Europe.

Kaiser Wilhelm II loved the armed forces. In this picture he is wearing a German army uniform.

The Kaiser had factories built, and increased production of coal, iron and steel. Most of the other great powers had empires overseas, so he decided that Germany should have one too – "a place in the sun," as he called it. For that, he needed a big navy.

This German steel plant was owned by the Krupp family. They produced weapons for Germany during the First World War.

In 1906, the British launched the first 'dreadnought' – a powerful new battleship. Soon, the Germans were building dreadnoughts too.

The French and Russians watched anxiously as Germany became more and more powerful. Meanwhile, the British worried about Wilhelm's growing fleet. Before long, all three nations had made agreements to help each other if Germany attacked them.

By 1907, there were two opposing groups of great powers in Europe, each suspicious of the other. On one side was Germany, Austria-Hungary and Italy. On the other side was Britain, France and Russia, who would later become known as the 'Allies'. Their opponents would be known as the 'Central Powers'.

Both sides were just as strong as each other, and most people believed that, because of this balance of power, no country would risk attacking another. After all, a war that involved all of the great powers was bound to plunge Europe into chaos and bloodshed.

This German map shows Germany and Austria-Hungary as brave soldiers, sandwiched between hostile nations – Britain, France and Russia.

British battleships loom on the horizon. When war broke out, the British Royal Navy had the largest fleet in the world.

Then, on Sunday, June 28, 1914, Archduke Franz Ferdinand was shot dead in Bosnia – part of the Austro-Hungarian Empire.

It didn't take long for the Austro-Hungarians to find out who was behind the murder. The assassins were from the Black Hand, a Serbian terrorist group. Serbia was an independent nation, which shared a border with Bosnia. The Black Hand believed that Bosnia should be part of Serbia, instead of Austria-Hungary.

Austro-Hungarian politicians were furious. They blamed the Serbian government, and sent them a list of demands. When these demands were not met, they declared war on Serbia.

Europe was thrown into crisis. The Russians supported Serbia. The Germans sided with Austria-Hungary. The French stood by the Russians. The great powers were drawn in one by one, like falling dominos.

The Italians and the British refused to commit to war. But for the other great powers, it was too late. By August, their armies were on the move, and the storm of war was about to break.

Chapter 3
Over by Christmas

In the cities of Europe, people cheered, waved flags and sang patriotic songs. They expected the fighting to be over by Christmas, with a glorious victory for their own nation. Some French soldiers even painted "See you in Berlin" on the trains that would carry them into battle.

Young Germans on their way to join the army and fight for their country

Meanwhile, anxious generals drew up battle plans. German commanders planned to invade France at once, capture Paris and turn back to meet the Russian army before it could even reach the German border. That way, they wouldn't have to fight both nations at once.

This strategy was called the 'Schlieffen Plan', after the general who came up with it. It was bold, but it had one big flaw. To reach France, the Germans had to march through Belgium – and the British had signed a treaty promising to protect it.

In the end, the Germans decided to gamble. As their chancellor remarked, surely the British wouldn't risk going to war for "a mere scrap of paper"?

Waves of German troops entered Belgium by train, supported by massive artillery guns, called 'Big Berthas', to pound the enemy into submission.

Then, the Germans got a nasty surprise. On August 4, they received an ultimatum from the British government: leave Belgium by midnight. If not, Britain would be at war with Germany. Midnight came, and the Germans sent no reply.

The next day, in Britain, thousands of young men lined up outside recruitment offices, impatient to cross the sea and fight the enemy.

Not everyone was so enthusiastic. Sir Edward Grey, the British Foreign Secretary, predicted that dark times lay ahead. "The lamps are going out all over Europe," he said sadly, "and we shall not see them lit again in our lifetime."

Railways helped to move men and equipment around very quickly. This German train is about to leave Berlin for Belgium.

Belgian cavalry (mounted soldiers) in Brussels, the capital of Belgium

The Germans had made a new enemy, but their Schlieffen Plan was working perfectly. To the south, they drove off a French attack on Germany. In Belgium, a small British force joined the defending troops, but couldn't stop the German onslaught.

Kaiser Wilhelm's army advanced into France and, by late August, terrified Parisians were packing up and fleeing the capital. It seemed as if the war would indeed be over by Christmas.

But German generals were receiving bad news from the east. The Austro-Hungarian army was stuck in battle with the Serbians. Worse still, the Russian army had moved faster than expected, and was bearing down on Germany.

The Germans had no choice but to split their forces in two. While the advance on Paris continued, part of the army hurried back through Germany to meet the Russians.

Led by an old veteran, General von Hindenburg, and energetic General Ludendorff, German troops surrounded and destroyed an enormous Russian force at the Battle of Tannenberg, to the east of Germany. They took more than 90,000 prisoners, and stopped the Russians in their tracks.

It was a fine victory, but it left the German forces near Paris weak and isolated.

This painting shows German commanders von Hindenburg (left) and Ludendorff (right) making plans for the Battle of Tannenberg.

French soldiers march by a column of taxis from Paris. The red in their uniform made them easy targets, so later, a pale blue uniform was introduced instead.

At the same time, the Allied forces in France were growing stronger. Most of the British army had now arrived, and French reinforcements were brought in by taxi cabs.

Determined to defend Paris, the Allies attacked along the Marne river, just outside the city. For the first time, they forced the Germans back.

Refusing to give up, German commanders sent their troops north, to march round and attack the enemy from behind. But Allied generals had the same idea, and sent their own troops north, too.

The two sides clashed near the coast in a brutal battle, at a place called Ypres. Big artillery guns boomed, and machine guns clattered, each one spitting out up to a hundred bullets per minute.

These weapons had been invented just before the war, and few people realized how deadly they would be. Tens of thousands of soldiers died at Ypres. But, despite these terrible losses, neither side managed to gain an advantage. It was a pattern that would be repeated many times in the years to come.

Many of the German soldiers killed at Ypres were just teenage volunteers. For their families, the battle became known as the 'Massacre of the Innocents'.

Big artillery guns, like these howitzers, killed more men than any other weapon in the war.

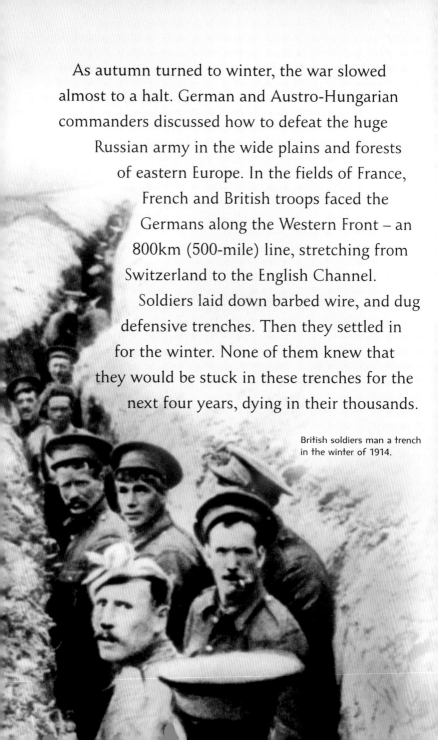

As autumn turned to winter, the war slowed almost to a halt. German and Austro-Hungarian commanders discussed how to defeat the huge Russian army in the wide plains and forests of eastern Europe. In the fields of France, French and British troops faced the Germans along the Western Front – an 800km (500-mile) line, stretching from Switzerland to the English Channel. Soldiers laid down barbed wire, and dug defensive trenches. Then they settled in for the winter. None of them knew that they would be stuck in these trenches for the next four years, dying in their thousands.

British soldiers man a trench in the winter of 1914.

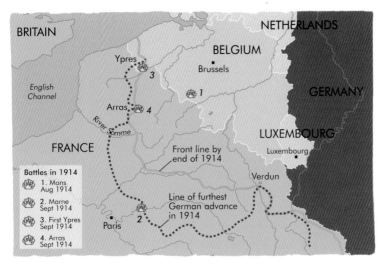

This map shows the fighting on the Western Front in late 1914.

The war wasn't over by Christmas, as everyone had hoped. But, on December 25, an extraordinary thing happened. On some parts of the Western Front, British and German troops cautiously emerged from their trenches to greet each other.

They met in no-man's-land – the crater-marked wasteland between the battle lines. Some played football, while others chatted, joked and even swapped gifts. For a single day, they were all comrades, in it together. But, by nightfall, the guns were firing once again.

Chapter 4
The world at war

"There is in Canada but one mind and one heart," declared the Prime Minister of Canada, when war broke out. "All Canadians are behind the mother country!"

Canada was part of the British Empire, and the 'mother country' meant Britain. All of the great powers had colonies scattered around the world, where local troops were preparing to fight for European masters. Some boarded ships, bound for the trenches in France, while others attacked nearby enemy colonies.

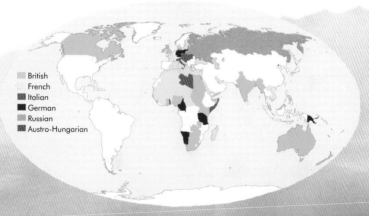

British
French
Italian
German
Russian
Austro-Hungarian

This map shows the empires of Europe's great powers in 1914.

Other nations entered the fray too, hoping to win new territory. In October 1914, Turkey joined the Central Powers. The Turks ruled over a crumbling empire, that contained people of several different nations, including Armenians and Arabs. Now the ambitious Turkish war leader, Enver Pasha, planned to restore this empire to its former glory.

Enver Pasha (right) salutes Kaiser Wilhelm II of Germany.

The British were especially worried. The main oil supplier for their navy was southern Persia, which was dangerously close to the Turkish Empire. So they hurriedly sent troops from India (a British colony at that time) to defend Persia.

This equipment was used to extract oil from the ground in Persia. The oil was vital fuel for British ships.

Enver Pasha was more interested in Russia, though, and sent a large force north to invade. He imagined conquering a vast new land for Turkey – but he hadn't counted on the brutal Russian winter. His troops had to march through freezing cold and blizzards, and when the Russians struck back, the Turkish army collapsed.

This map shows the Turkish Empire.

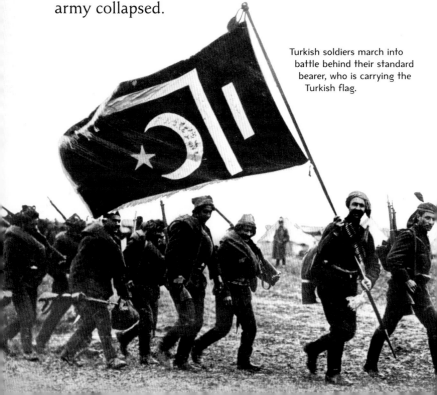

Turkish soldiers march into battle behind their standard bearer, who is carrying the Turkish flag.

Furious, Enver looked around for someone to blame. He settled on the Armenians. They were Turkish subjects who were Christian, not Muslim, like the Turks. Some of them had supported the Russians.

Armenians were forced to leave their homes and travel miles across the desert to prison camps.

In revenge, Enver ordered his men to round up Armenian men, women and children. These people were driven to camps, where they were worked to death, or simply shot.

Around 800,000 Armenians died from Enver Pasha's terrible persecution.

Meanwhile, Winston Churchill, a British politician in charge of the Royal Navy, came up with a bold plan to defeat the Turks. He hoped to capture the Gallipoli Peninsula in Turkey, and then strike at the Turkish capital, Constantinople.

The Gallipoli Peninsula was in the western part of the Turkish Empire.

In April 1915, a large Allied force, including British, French, Indian and ANZAC (Australian and New Zealand Army Corps) soldiers, attacked Gallipoli. But the peninsula was extremely well defended, and the attackers couldn't get a foothold.

The fighting in Gallipoli dragged on for months, with no progress. Summer brought stifling heat, flies and disease. Winter brought flooding, frostbite and pneumonia. The Allies finally gave up in December.

In the same month, the Turks managed to trap a British force in Mesopotamia (present-day Iraq), in the town of Kut-al-Amara. The British troops had to surrender the following year, which added to the humiliation of the failure in Gallipoli.

This painting, by an Australian war artist, shows ANZAC troops scrambling up a hillside in Gallipoli to attack the Turks.

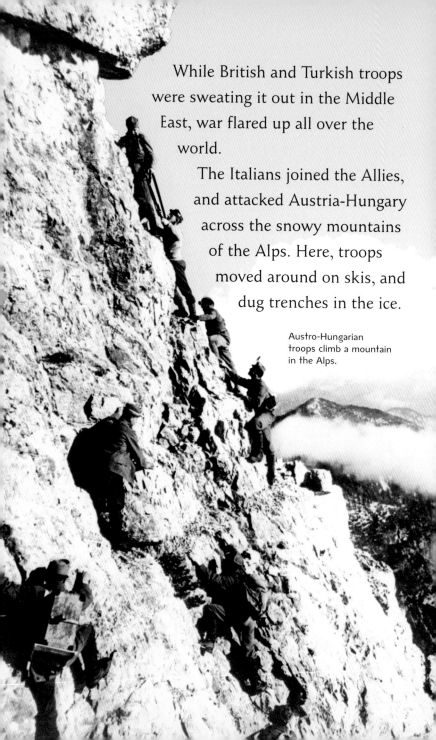

While British and Turkish troops were sweating it out in the Middle East, war flared up all over the world.

The Italians joined the Allies, and attacked Austria-Hungary across the snowy mountains of the Alps. Here, troops moved around on skis, and dug trenches in the ice.

Austro-Hungarian troops climb a mountain in the Alps.

In the skies above the Western Front, fighter plane pilots battled in 'dogfights', shooting at each other with machine guns.

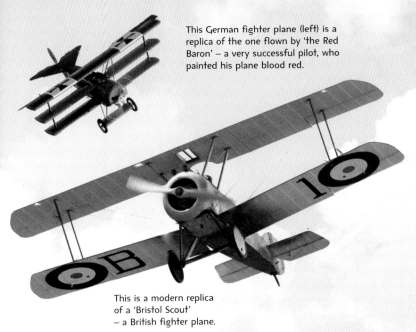

This German fighter plane (left) is a replica of the one flown by 'the Red Baron' – a very successful pilot, who painted his plane blood red.

This is a modern replica of a 'Bristol Scout' – a British fighter plane.

The Japanese entered the war in August 1914, declaring war on Germany. They seized enemy colonies in the Pacific Ocean, and captured a large German naval base at Tsingtao in China.

Without a base, the German ships were forced to roam the seas, attacking Allied vessels whenever they got a chance.

German admirals had other problems too. The British Royal Navy was patrolling the North Sea, stopping supply ships from getting into Germany, and warships from getting out.

In the North Sea, as well as the Pacific, the German navy was reduced to sneak attacks on enemy ships and ports. There was one big naval battle at Jutland in 1916. But, even though the German fleet sank more ships than the British, they were outgunned and had to retreat.

There was some hope for them, though. While the British ruled the waves, the Germans ruled the sea beneath. They used submarines called *unterseeboote* (under-water boats), or U-boats, to sink Allied supply ships.

A U-boat emerges from the freezing waters of the North Sea.

On May 7, 1915, a U-boat attacked and sank the *RMS Lusitania*, a passenger liner carrying civilians. 1,198 people drowned, causing outrage all over the world.

Among the victims were 128 US citizens. Many angry Americans called for their President, Woodrow Wilson, to declare war on Germany.

The Germans were playing a dangerous game. If the Americans entered the war, it could tip the scales against them.

An American newspaper and a French book report the sinking of the *Lusitania*.

Chapter 5

A numbers game

In Europe, it had begun to seem as if the fighting could go on forever.

On the Eastern Front, the Russians poured more and more men into battle, with no success. "At times," wrote Field Marshal von Hindenburg, "we had to remove the piles of enemy bodies from before our trenches, so as to get a clear field of fire against new waves of assault."

The Germans won several victories, but the Russian army was too big to overcome completely. Neither side could gain the upper hand.

On the Western Front, there was a grim stalemate. Battles lasted months, ended with terrible casualties and achieved almost nothing.

The problem was that new weapons made it easy to defend a trench, but hard to attack one.

Austro-Hungarian cavalry
patrol the Eastern Front.

In the past, battles were won quickly by glorious
charges of infantry (soldiers who fought on foot)
and cavalry (who fought on horseback).

  But in the First World War, advancing infantry
soldiers were cut down by hails of machine gun
bullets. Meanwhile, artillery guns fired exploding
bits of metal, called shells. They churned fields
into muddy wastelands, making cavalry
charges impossible.

These German soldiers are wearing gas
masks. Some types of gas were used
as deadly weapons, blinding victims
or choking them to death.

Generals, politicians and scientists struggled to find new tactics or technology to break the deadlock. But meanwhile, soldiers on the front line had to sit it out, their comrades dying around them day by day.

Many trenches were no better than ditches, infested with lice and rats – some as big as cats. In summer, there was a constant stench of toilets and rotting bodies, and in winter, there was endless cold, rain and mud. Soldiers shivered in 'dugouts' – cramped holes in the ground where they slept. Many caught frostbite, fever or 'trench foot' – a painful infection caused by the damp, that made their feet swell up and turn black.

A lot of the time, life was very boring, with days spent dozing, or writing letters back home. But danger was always there.

This British soldier is eating his dinner in a trench.

Shell explosions threw clouds of earth into the air.

Soldiers known as snipers watched enemy trenches and shot anything that moved. Cannons called mortars launched explosive shells high into the air, to come screaming down on the enemy. Every soldier dreaded the roar of the artillery most of all. It shook the earth and tore men limb from limb.

At night, patrols sneaked out to repair trenches and replace barbed wire, under cover of darkness. Sometimes they went on missions into no-man's-land to spy on the enemy, or carry out raids.

If these soldiers met the enemy, they were supposed to attack with blades, called bayonets, attached to the end of their rifles. But some found shovels, homemade clubs or knives more effective.

Flares were sometimes used to light up no-man's-land at night.

Most officers fought in the trenches with their men. But some commanders set up headquarters in French country houses, miles behind the front line. They ate three-course dinners with silver cutlery, and drank fine wine from crystal glasses. In the afternoons, they went riding or shooting.

By 1915, many of these commanders had decided that if they could only throw enough shells and men at the enemy forces, they would overwhelm them and win a glorious victory. This idea would cost the lives of thousands.

British and French leaders meet in 1916. They are (left to right) General Joffre, President Pointcaré, King George V, General Foch and General Haig.

German infantry soldiers wait by a roadside, on their way to the Battle of Verdun.

In early 1916, the German commander, General von Falkenhayn, came up with a plan to attack a French fortress at Verdun. He hoped that the French would bring most of their army there to defend it, allowing him to destroy their forces with artillery fire.

To von Falkenhayn, it was a simple numbers game. If he could kill three French soldiers for every German he lost, the enemy would have no choice but to surrender. In his own words, he would "bleed France white".

General von Falkenhayn

Verdun was a death trap, just as von Falkenhayn had hoped. Hundreds of thousands of men were killed – so many that the battle became known as the 'Mincing Machine'. But even though the French suffered more than the Germans, their commander, Pétain, doggedly stood his ground. "They shall not pass," he told his superiors.

Months later, the German line had barely moved forward at all. General von Falkenhayn was replaced by Field Marshal von Hindenburg, who ended the slaughter.

This image, from a French film, shows a French soldier being hit by a bullet at the Battle of Verdun.

While the Germans were busy at Verdun, the British commander, Douglas Haig, hoped to break through their line further north, at the River Somme. He was sure it would be 'the big push' that would crush the 'Boche'

A portrait of Douglas Haig

(a nickname for the Germans) and win the war.

First, he ordered a massive bombardment of the enemy trenches, lasting a full week. Then at 7:30 in the morning on July 1, the barrage stopped. In the sudden silence, Haig's men went 'over the top' – they clambered out of their trenches to attack.

British soldiers called sappers dug under no-man's-land before the battle. They laid explosive devices, called mines, under German positions. This photograph shows one of the mines exploding.

British soldiers attack at the Battle of the Somme. This image is from a British film made during the battle.

Haig was convinced that his artillery had completely broken the Germans. He planned for his troops to occupy the enemy trenches. Then a large cavalry force would ride right into the heart of Germany.

But, in fact, the 'Boche' were safe inside bunkers and dugouts, deep beneath the earth. As the British troops walked across no-man's-land, the Germans emerged from hiding and opened fire with machine guns.

The battle was a massacre. On the first day, around 20,000 men were killed, and 40,000 wounded. By November, thousands more had died. When the smoke cleared, the 'big push' hadn't won the war – just a few miles of muddy ground.

Even after the Somme, Haig was still determined to win a glorious victory. The following year, he launched an offensive to capture U-boat bases on the coast of Belgium. The attack descended into chaos near the village of Passchendaele. Heavy rain and the explosions of shells turned the battlefield into a wet, muddy swamp. Many men sank below the surface forever.

For some, the waste of life was too much to bear. A British officer, Siegfried Sassoon, wrote a poem about the battle, from the point of view of a dead soldier. "I died in hell," he wrote. "They called it Passchendaele."

These Australian soldiers have laid down wooden 'duckboards' to cross the swampy ground at Passchendaele.

Chapter 6
The Home Front

The noise of the Somme carried far behind the front line, and one explosion could even be heard in London. This distant roar reminded civilians of fathers, brothers and sons who might not come home. Every day, people scoured casualty lists in the newspapers, praying not to see the name of a relative.

When the war began, most people didn't realize how much it would affect them. But in some countries it became horribly real. The Germans burned down houses in Belgium, and executed men, women and children. In 1915, the Austro-Hungarians marched into Serbia, forcing civilians to flee to Greece and Albania.

The great powers suffered too. Allied naval blockades caused food shortages in Germany and Austria-Hungary, forcing the governments to ration the little they had. In return, German ships shelled British coastal towns, while their planes

At night, searchlights hunted for enemy planes and zeppelins, so they could be shot down with anti-aircraft guns.

and airships, called zeppelins, bombed cities.

This was the world's first 'total war' – a conflict which sucked in civilians as well as soldiers. They helped out in villages, towns and cities behind the front line. This was known as the Home Front.

These houses in Burton-on-Trent, Britain, have been bombed by German zeppelins.

Politicians everywhere knew that the Home Front was vital to success on the battlefield. Armies used up large amounts of food, ammunition and artillery shells, and it was up to workers at home to keep them supplied.

In many countries, men were forced to fight – a process called conscription. So, for the first time in a war, women went in large numbers to work in factories, making shells and weapons to be sent to the front line. "If the women in the factories stopped work for twenty minutes," declared French commander Joffre, "the Allies would lose the war."

This woman is making a propeller for a fighter plane in a factory, in England.

It was important to keep people's spirits up, too. Streets were plastered with posters, encouraging men to join the army, and explaining why the war had to be won. Official photographers sent home pictures from the battlefields that made the fighting look heroic.

Meanwhile, newspapers printed

One of the war's most famous posters shows Lord Kitchener, a British war hero, appealing to British men to join the army.

positive, patriotic articles. "Everything has gone well!" announced the headline in a British paper, after the first day of the Battle of the Somme. Even private letters, sent home from soldiers in the trenches, were carefully read by officers. Any sentences which revealed too much were deleted.

No one heard about the real horrors of trench warfare, and no one saw the fields full of dead, rotting bodies.

Even far behind the front lines, people were terrified that enemies were lurking among them: foreign spies. In Germany, visitors from Allied countries were rounded up and imprisoned. In Britain, Germans and Austro-Hungarians were held captive on the Isle of Man. New laws were brought in to restrict access to telephones, and anyone suspected of being a spy was arrested.

People were right to be suspicious. Secret agents operated everywhere, finding out about enemy battle plans, and sending messages back to their own countries, written in code. In Room 40 of the Admiralty Building in London, the British assembled a team to work on cracking German codes. There were mathematicians, translators and even crossword champions. Their work would change the course of the war.

Margareta Zelle, also known as Mata Hari, was a dancer who spied for both Germany and France. In 1917, the French had her executed because of her work for the Germans.

Chapter 7
Endgame

In January 1917, agents at Room 40 intercepted a coded telegram. It had been sent from the German foreign minister, Arthur Zimmerman, to his ambassador in Mexico. Once the codebreakers deciphered it, they knew they had struck gold.

In the telegram, Zimmerman ordered the ambassador to try to form an alliance with Mexico and Japan, against the United States. The British passed the telegram on to the Americans. They were sure that it would bring the USA into the war against Germany.

This is the 'Zimmerman Telegram' that brought the USA into the war. It is written in a code made up of numbers.

932.29   WWI DOCUMENT: ZIMMERMAN TELEGRAM, 1917.
Credit: The Granger Collection, New York

The Americans were outraged by the telegram. They were already furious with Germany for its U-boat attacks, and this was the final straw. In April 1917, US President Wilson announced that his country was at war with Germany.

Help was on its way – and just in time. In May, French troops began to disobey orders, after their commanders sent them on yet another disastrous offensive. In September, a massive Russian attack on the Eastern Front came to a standstill.

This poster urges Americans to join the army before they are 'drafted' – forced to join.

The Russian people had had enough. There was a revolution, and the government was overthrown. Then, in December, the country's new leaders signed an agreement with Germany to stop the fighting on the Eastern Front.

Time was running out for the Central Powers. They had to defeat France and Britain before American forces arrived. But the collapse of the Russian army gave them hope. General Ludendorff decided to throw everything he had into a colossal assault on the Western Front. This became known as the 'Spring Offensive'. It would either win the war for Germany, or lose it.

American soldiers – who were nicknamed 'doughboys' – parade through the streets of New York.

On March 21, 1918, German artillery roared into life, and storm troopers – the best soldiers in the German army – scrambled out of their trenches.

They raced forward, hurling grenades and unleashing scorching bursts of fire from flamethrowers. Their orders were to smash through enemy positions and keep on moving, while the rest of the army followed.

German storm troopers rush towards the Allied trenches on the Western Front.

This ferocious assault drove the Allied troops back, and seriously alarmed their commanders. "Each one of us must fight on to the end," Haig told his men.

In Germany, people thought that victory was in sight. But, although the army had advanced a long way, it had lost a lot of men. Those who remained were exhausted and stranded in enemy territory, far away from their artillery and supplies.

Every day, more US soldiers were arriving in the trenches. Allied generals, united under a French commander, Marshal Foch, decided it was time to turn the tables.

A British artillery gun opens fire on the Germans during the Spring Offensive.

This photograph shows a British tank being blown apart by German shells. In the background, another tank is advancing with a group of British soldiers.

The British struck back on August 8, near the city of Amiens. First, their gunners used new targeting techniques to pinpoint the German artillery. Then they fired a rapid barrage of shells, wiping out the enemy guns before the battle had even begun.

Next, British soldiers attacked, supported by aircraft and new metal-plated vehicles called tanks, which had only been developed over the last few years. At the same time, British artillery kept firing, aiming their shells to land just in front of the advancing British troops. This 'creeping barrage' moved towards the enemy, always just ahead of the British forces.

After years of failed offensives, this combination of tactics, technology and firepower finally paid off. British forces smashed through the German line. Even General Ludendorff had to admit that it was a "black day" for his army.

Amiens was just the beginning. Sensing victory, the Allies kept attacking and advancing, pushing on towards Germany.

British tanks going forward after the Battle of Amiens. The tanks are carrying 'cribs' on top. Cribs were for lowering into ditches, so that the tanks could cross them safely.

British soldiers enter the French city of Lille in October 1918.

For the Germans, things went from bad to worse, as a deadly flu virus spread through their ranks. With fresh American troops arriving all the time, it seemed as if the war was as good as finished.

Meanwhile, Allied troops reached the Hindenburg Line – a German system of concrete bunkers, trenches and fortifications.

German commanders had once believed the Hindenburg Line was invincible. But they were soon proved wrong. Allied shells battered the fortifications day and night, while troops and tanks attacked on the ground. It was all too much for the Germans. Within four days, Allied forces were pouring through the broken line.

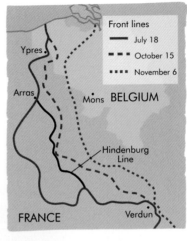

Allied advances in late 1918

This painting shows an attack on the Hindenburg Line.

Constantinople

TURKISH EMPIRE

PERSIA

Cairo

Arab
attacks

British
advance

British
advance

Arabian
Peninsula

EGYPT

This map shows the offensives against Turkey in 1918.

While the German army fell apart, the Turkish Empire was overwhelmed by enemies on all sides. A brilliant British commander, Sir Edmund 'The Bull' Allenby, attacked from Egypt and invaded the western part of the empire. At the same time, the Turks faced another British offensive in the east, and a rebellion by Arabs, who wanted to break away from the Turkish Empire. With the help of a British officer, T. E. Lawrence, the Arabs ambushed Turkish troops and supply lines, before disappearing into the desert.

T. E. Lawrence, sometimes known as 'Lawrence of Arabia', took this photograph of Arab troops in the desert.

A Turkish soldier surrenders to the British in early 1918.

By late October 1918, Turkish forces were in collapse, and had to surrender.

Meanwhile, the Austro-Hungarian Empire was disintegrating, as its subject nations demanded independence and an end to the fighting. Finally, the Italians managed to break through the Alps, and pressed on into Austria.

On October 29, the German navy refused to continue fighting. There were riots in the streets of Germany, and the country was on the brink of chaos. German politicians and generals had to swallow the bitter truth: the war was lost. It was time to admit defeat.

Chapter 8
The war to end all wars

On a frosty morning, November 11, 1918, a group of German politicians and officers met Marshal Foch in a railway carriage, in a forest behind the Allied lines. There they signed an armistice: an agreement to stop fighting.

At 11 o'clock that morning – "the eleventh hour of the eleventh day of the eleventh month" – the First World War came to an end.

Church bells rang out across Europe. In cities, many people waved flags and cheered. Others wept. The war had been won, but only at an incredible, appalling cost of life.

These are the British and French men who signed the armistice, standing by the railway carriage. Marshal Foch is second from the right.

Kaiser Wilhelm II had left Germany for Holland two days earlier. He was furious, convinced that he had been betrayed by his generals, who he thought could have fought on and won the war.

He was not alone. Most Germans didn't understand what had happened on the Western Front. Their country hadn't been invaded, so why did they have to make peace?

Soldiers and civilians in London celebrate the end of the war.

British Prime Minister
David Lloyd George
(left), French Prime
Minister Georges
Clemenceau (middle)
and US President
Woodrow Wilson

In Paris, Allied leaders debated what to do with
the defeated Germans. The French Prime Minister,
Clemenceau, wanted to punish them so that they
could never start a war again. But US President
Wilson thought that being generous would help
to keep the peace in future.

After months of argument, they came to a
compromise. In the Palace of Versailles, near Paris,
they presented German politicians with a treaty
to sign.

When the Germans found out what the terms were, they were horrified. They had to pay the Allies vast sums of money, known as reparations. More humiliating still, they had to accept the blame for starting the war. On June 28, 1919, they reluctantly signed the Treaty of Versailles.

At last, there was peace – but the war had changed the world. Borders were redrawn, and some countries became independent for the first time. The Middle East was mostly divided between Britain and France, which angered the Arabs, who had been promised their own independent country. Russia had a new revolutionary government, and the Turkish and Austro-Hungarian Empires were both gone forever.

This map shows Europe's new borders, after the First World War.

Some soldiers had no jobs to come home to. This disabled German officer is begging on the streets of Berlin.

It wasn't just nations that had changed. For those who'd fought and killed, or lost loved ones, life could never be the same again. Many felt betrayed by the governments and generals who had sent so many men to die. Some ex-soldiers thought that they had more in common with their so-called enemies, the men they had fought in the trenches, than with their own rulers.

The Salvation Army provides food for poor citizens of Berlin in the 1920s.

In Germany, the payment of reparations caused terrible poverty, and many people were angry. One of them was a man named Adolf Hitler. He had fought in the war, and told anyone who would listen that the Treaty of Versailles was wrong.

Even among the victors, there were those who agreed with him. Others said that the treaty wasn't harsh enough, and Germany would soon be able to start another war. "This is not a peace," Marshal Foch predicted. "It is an armistice for 20 years."

He was right. Just 20 years after 'the war to end all wars', Hitler would bring about an even more destructive conflict: the Second World War.

Adolf Hitler salutes German storm troopers in the city of Nuremberg in 1938. On his arm he wears the Swastika – the symbol of his party, the Nazis.

The First World War was one of the greatest disasters in the history of the world. It drew in 28 countries, and caused the deaths of around 21 million people.

At eleven o'clock on November 11, 1919 – one year since the end of the war – there were two minutes of silence, to show respect for the dead. A British journalist wrote about what he saw and felt that day.

"An elderly woman, not far away, wiped her eyes, and the man beside her looked white and

After the fighting stopped, poppies grew in many parts of the Western Front. Today, the poppy is a symbol of those who died in the war.

stern… it was a silence which was almost pain… and the spirit of memory brooded over it all."

Today, memorials stand throughout the world to the victims of the war. In many countries, November 11 is Remembrance Day – a time to think of those who died.

A British general salutes a war memorial in London, in 1925. Memorials were put up all over Britain.

Index

Usborne Quicklinks

You can find out more about the First World War by going to the Usborne Quicklinks Website at www.usborne.com/quicklinks and typing in the keywords 'yr first world war'.
Please note Usborne Publishing cannot be responsible for the content of any website other than its own.